A TELEPHONE CALL FROM CLEVELAND

A Memoir

Dominic Di Giamarino

authorHOUSE®

AuthorHouse™
1663 Liberty Drive
Bloomington, IN 47403
www.authorhouse.com
Phone: 1 (800) 839-8640

Published by AuthorHouse 10/19/2016

ISBN: 978-1-5246-3811-5 (sc)
ISBN: 978-1-5246-3809-2 (hc)
ISBN: 978-1-5246-3810-8 (e)

Library of Congress Control Number: 2016914679

Print information available on the last page.

Any people depicted in stock imagery provided by Thinkstock are models, and such images are being used for illustrative purposes only. Certain stock imagery © Thinkstock.

This book is printed on acid-free paper.

CONTENTS

PROLOGUE

While running alongside the fast moving freight, I reached for the metal ladder and swung my right foot up to catch the bottom rung. My shoe slipped and suddenly my foot was within an inch of the freight car's grinding wheel. As a young kid I had hopped many freights, but this time, I knew I was in deep trouble. I would have to rely on my upper-body strength to get me through this, but at age ten, I was just a puny, little kid. My body was dripping with sweat as I tried to pull myself from harm's way, knowing that if I were to let go, the result would be tragic. Amputation, if not death! Boy, would my parents be angry.

Somehow, I was able to muster the necessary strength to lift myself from danger and to this day, I could not tell you where the added muscle came from. I signaled my pal Joey, who had hopped the previous coal car, and we were on our way to our favorite swimming hole. It seems like my early years were challenged with a number of "situations" that could have caused me great bodily harm but I guess someone up there really liked me. I was truly blessed with an exciting and wonderful childhood.

My story begins in a small, coal mining town in eastern Pennsylvania called Mahanoy City (pronounced MA-ha-noy) and I will try to share some interesting, humorous, and unforgettable memories of my early years as a skinny, Italian kid growing up during the 1940's. I was the first born to Eddie, a hard-working, hard drinking father and Genny, the greatest mother (and cook) in the world. I will also introduce you to The Di Labio's, The Polidore's, and The Di Giamarino's, better known as "The Family."

I would like to thank my parents for providing me and my sister with a loving environment while going through so many difficult times of their own, and also acknowledge them for applying the necessary punishment when needed and the praise when earned. You taught us well.

Finally, a sincere thank you to Joey and Louie Fazio who, over the years, have repeatedly urged me to continue this project. They have certainly served as an invaluable extension of my memory and without them, this story may never have been told.

ACKNOWLEDGMENTS

❖ ❖ ❖

The author would like to thank: Paul Coombe, from the Mahanoy Area Historical Society, for keeping me on the 'straight and narrow' when it came to the historical facts of this project.

Family members and friends, who for years had heard about 'the book' . . . and will now finally get to read it.

Christopher Maughan, an author himself, for giving me that 'positive push' whenever I needed it.

My daughter Tami, for helping me hurdle this quagmire called 'self-publishing.'

My granddaughter Jackie, for typing that 'final draft.'

And finally, to the members of the cast that made my early years . . . a pleasure.

THE FAMILY TREE

Mom's Family

Guiseppe Di Labio

Graziella (Garofalo)

    Antonio

    Mary

    Anna

  Genevieve (Mom)

    Ernesto (Ernie)

    Alfredo (Babe)

Dad's Family

Domenico Di Giamarino

Marianna (Pillo)

  Catherine (Katy)

    Lena

    Frank

  Edward (Dad)

  James (Jimmy)

My Family

Edward Di Giamarino

Genevieve (Di Labio)

  Dominic (Sonny)

    Palma

Dad's (Adopted) Family

Antonio Polidore

Annunciata (Pillo)

Mary

Alva

Anna

Ida

Irene

Stella

Edward (Dad)

Dante (Danny)

Paul

Emma

Florence (Flossie)

Alfredo (Freddie)

GRANDPAP-GIUSEPPE
DI LABIO

GRANDMAM-GRAZIELLA
DI LABIO

GRANDMA-ANNUNCIATA
POLIDORE

GRANDPA-ANTONIO
POLIDORE

GRANDPAP & AUNT ANNIE
DI LABIO

UNCLE BABE DI LABIO

MOM-GENNY DI LABIO

UNCLE ERNIE
DI LABIO

GRANDMAM GRAZIELLA DI LABIO

ANNIE, GRANDMAM, & MARY DI LABIO

GRANDMAM DI LABIO (GAROFALO)

A LITTLE HISTORY

In the early 1900's, the families of my parents migrated from their native land of Italy; Mom's group from the Province of Chieti, in the Region of Abruzzi and Dad's from the Province of Campobasso, in the Region of Molise. The Di Labio's, (Mom's group) settled into the coal mining region of Eastern Pennsylvania while my Dad's birth family (the Di Giamarino's) located to West Virginia. My Dad's adopted family, (the Polidore's), also from the Province of Campobasso, hung their shingle in Shenandoah,Pennsylvania which was about four miles from the Di Labio's in Mahanoy City.

My father was about three years old when he lost both of his parents to the influenza epidemic of 1917-18, and it was decided that he and his siblings would be taken in by other family members rather than the option of an orphanage. Annunciata Polidore, my Dad's birth mother's sister, elected to take my father, Edward, even though, she had six children of her own. In short order, his biological siblings went to other family members who were residing in and around Camden, New Jersey.

Dad dropped out of school in the sixth grade and went to work at the St. Nicholas Coal Breaker (near Shenandoah) with his new father, Tony, to bring in a little extra money for the family. Until my Dad entered his life, Grandpa Polidore had

7

only female off-spring, so I'm guessing that he was kinda glad to finally have a son he could teach the coal business to. As time went on, Eddie met Genny, Eddie married Genny . . . and along came me.

EDDIE DI GIAMARINO
1926

GENNY DI LABIO
1928

DAD, MOM, GRANDMAM, & ME

MOM, DAD & ME   MOM, GRANDMAM,
                       AUNT MARY, & ME

MOM, GRANDMAM, PALMA, & ME

GRANDPA POLIDORE & DAD   FRIEND & GRANDMAM
                                DI LABIO

SAINT NICHOLAS BREAKER

PALMA, MOM, LITTLE ERNIE,
& AUNT DOROTHY

GRANDMAM &
UNCLE BABE

ME AT OUR HOUSE ON EAST SOUTH ST.

AUNT MARY DI LABIO

DAD, MOM, & ME-
MAHANOY CITY

DAD & THE POLIDORE GIRLS

IN THE BEGINNING

On March 12, 1936, yours truly made his entrance. It was a cold, wintry day, and the road to Locust Mountain Hospital was covered with snow and ice. Because of the extreme weather, Dad's Model A Ford was unable to navigate the mountainous terrain, and we were forced to return to Mahanoy City to acquire the assistance of one of my Mom's cousins, Gustine Di Labio, and his much heavier and more capable 1935 Packard. Eventually, we got through, but I'm sure it was no picnic.

In later years Mom explained it was a complicated birth, and I was what they then called an "instrument" baby. I was not willing to enter the world at that particular time so the doctor had to use surgical forceps to help me complete the journey. Luckily, it hasn't affect . . . affect . . . a bothered me at all.

My memory of those formative years is a bit vague, but I do remember being treated as "the little king." I was christened Dominic Edward Di Giamarino and answered to the family name, Sonny, and my friends called me D.G. As the oldest son, I was adored by my parents and when it came to grandparents, aunts and uncles . . . I could do no wrong. I was in complete control, that is until my sister Palma came along, when I was about seven. The limelight seemed to dim a bit, and I remember thinking, *I would have rather had a puppy. This kid couldn't even fetch a ball!*

Our family was off to a good start and even though we didn't have an abundance of money . . . we all seemed content and agreeable with our station in life.

Incidentally, Locust Mountain Hospital is now a long-term care facility. Do you think there's a chance I could end up where I began?

GENNY & EDDIE

PALMA

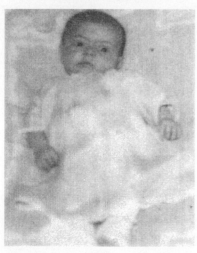

ME

MOM, DAD, & ME   PALMA & MOM

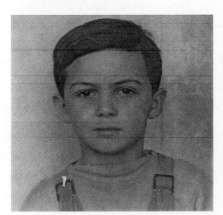

ME, AGAIN   DAD-SATURDAY NIGHT

MOM, DAD, PALMA, & ME AND OUR 1930
MODEL 'A' FORD IN BROCKTON, PA.

12TH STREET SCHOOL

❖❖❖

On the corner of 12th Street and East Pine, a three-story brick building, surrounded by large maple trees and wrought iron fencing was the focal point for my introduction to academia and society. It housed grades one through eight and the mission was to prepare each student for high school, college, and life. They even taught the Palmer Method of cursive writing. Theirs was a serious mission. There was no kindergarten or junior high back then, but it all seemed to work well. Most of the teachers were female, unmarried and deeply involved in their profession. As I look back, Misses Pounder, Jenkins, Williams, and Gallagher were phenomenal at what they did. If you didn't learn, it was on you. And how about Ms. Northey. Once we found out that her brother Ron played Major League Baseball for the St. Louis Browns, we automatically listened to every word she said.

Phillips, Heckler, Seddon, and Richards. Sounds like a law firm but, in fact, they were just a few of the renegades I used to run the streets with. The Fazio Brothers could have been a men's clothing chain but they were simply my partners-in-crime. Me, Donny Heckler, and the Fazio boys were inseparable and always looking for trouble . . . not the trouble of today mind you, but more like mischief. Donny had every comic book ever published and, at times, thought he was Superman. Sometimes he was, but not on the day he jumped from the roof of a South Street garage and broke his arm. I must tell you though, after it healed, he tried again (with cape), and he made it! Further proof that if you want to succeed, you must try, try again.

Joey and Louie: The Fazio Brothers. Almost every day, around recess time, an old Italian guy (about my current age) would push his fruit cart past our school, and Joey would keep him occupied while me and Louie would heist a few apples from the opposite side. If we could get enough of them we would sell them to the starving students who were less fortunate than ourselves. One could say that we were working on our business acumen. But one day, while we were doing our thing, Principal Weldon caught our act through her office window and soon requested our presence. I mean, what could she do? Kill us! Basically, we were good kids and responsible, too.

In fact, we were patrol boys: Traffic monitors that helped the younger kids cross the streets safely. That year, we did such a good job the school was going to sponsor us for a train trip to Philadelphia to see a Major League baseball game . . . maybe the Yankees and the Athletics! Yep, you guessed it . . . she punched our tickets, and there would be no ball game for us. Come to think of it, no more apples either. Well, not by the school yard anyhow.

I'll never forget the day the principal called my classroom and asked Ms. Jenkins to send me to her office ASAP. I immediately thought, *Now what did I do?* Turns out I didn't do anything wrong, but I did have a couple of visitors. This one had me snowed? She opened the door to her stockroom and there stood two of my favorite uncles, Freddie and Babe, in full military dress. They had just returned from Europe (WWII) and thought they would surprise me. Indeed they did. It seemed like they were gone for ages. Ms. Weldon asked if I would like to show them around the school (which both had previously attended), and that was an affirmative. This was so cool . . . even before there was cool!

12th Street School is no longer there, but many thanks to those magnificent teachers and the excellent education they provided for my life's journey. I, too, became an educator, and hopefully was able to touch a student or two as they had touched me. And in addition, a special thank you to whomever made the brilliant decision to annually broadcast the World Series games over the school public address system.

That was great!

12th STREET BUILDING

Mahanoy City, Pennsylvania

12th Street School

Miss Pounder
1st Grade

Miss Powell
2nd Grade

Miss Williams
3rd Grade

Miss Brennan
4th Grade

Miss Murphy
Kindergarten

Miss Edwards
5th Grade

Miss Weldon
Principal &
6th Grade

ME

MOM, GRANDMAM, PETE
GERBASI, & DOT. PALMA,
ME, LITTLE ERNIE, &
DONNY HECKLER

ME

& ME

ME & MY GODFATHER-
PETE GERBASI

CHURCHES AND SALOONS

The competition for the coal miner's soul was fierce. The Lord giveth the churches and the devil, well, he gave the saloons. In the 1940's, the borough of Mahanoy City had a population of approximately 14,000 people, 30 churches, and about 50 neighborhood saloons. Adukaiti's, Marina's, Matty Witmer's, and eventually, the Garze Brothers. And that was just on my block! To the best of my memory, Mom did the church thing, and Dad did saloons. Almost every day, late in the afternoon, Mom would say, "Sonny, go get your father for supper." She didn't even have to tell me where to go! I would jump on my bike, head for Adukaiti's and bingo, there he was, perched on a bar stool, complete with coal miner's cap and full black face. As I gazed through the thick, secondhand smoke, he and his buddies all appeared to look alike. It was spooky! I once asked him why he stopped at the saloon every night, and he replied, "Well it's like this, working in the mines all day, a lot of coal dust builds up in your throat, and it takes a stiff shot (or two) of good whiskey to get that stuff outta there." Well, I bought it . . . but I don't think my Mom ever did.

I loved Adukaiti's. Everyone knew me there, and the minute I walked in I was greeted with, "Eh Sonny, get up here . . . Sam, get this kid some potato chips and a soda." I even got to keep score at the many dart tournaments they used to have. My Dad was a lefty and a great dart thrower. Occasionally, they challenged other saloons and whoever lost, bought the booze. I remember beer was 5 cents a glass and the food on the bar was free . . . stuff like deviled eggs, pickled pig's feet, Polish sausage, and fried baloney sandwiches. By the time I got my Dad out of there, neither of us were very hungry, but to keep peace in the family, we ate anyhow. What a fun place Adukaiti's was! I learned how to shoot darts, had access to free food and drink, and picked up on a whole lot of grown-up words that I could never use around the house. It just didn't get much better than that.

In the late 40s, the Garze Brothers bought Adukaiti's and turned it into a saloon and pizzeria. They opened up the back room to families for dining and that did not go over too well with the serious, "men only" boys. My Dad moved his business over to Marina's and Witmer's and so did most of the miners that he worked with. Now I'd have to look for him in two places! Even though "the boys" didn't like it, Garze Brothers took off like a rocket. I guess the women were getting a little tired of cooking supper for the miners who never showed, because soon these women were taking their kids to Garze's, enjoying someone else's cooking, and having themselves a glass of beer as well. Yes, pay back is a bitch!

Like I said earlier, Mom did the church thing, and she had the pick of the lot when it came to religion. This little berg was totally saturated with houses of worship including Roman Catholic, Greek and Russian Orthodox, Protestant, Jewish, and the Byzantines.

My family was Roman Catholic, and our church was on the corner of 14th and East Pine Street. Mom attended most Sundays, Dad very seldom, and I, when Mom could catch me. We had a mean looking, old priest from Italy and his name was Father Negro. He said all the masses in Latin and Italian, and if you weren't an immigrant, you didn't know what he was talking about. Then, in or around 1945, a breath of fresh air blew into Sacred Heart Church in the form of one Father Anthony Mattrazzo.

He was young, also Italian (but spoke English), and was able to communicate with the juveniles. He soon began to draw the younger folks to his sermons and the Sunday attendance began to swell. This guy was cool. Okay, so let me tell you how cool he was.

One evening, when I was about ten . . . me, Joey Fazio, Pauley Phillips, and Donny Heckler were sitting on the curb, under a street light, near the corner of 12th and East Pine. Donny pulled out a big, glossy magazine that belonged to his older brother and said, "Hey you guys . . . take a look at this." Occasionally, he would bring out some of his comic books, but this one was different. This magazine was loaded with a variety of colored photos showing scantily clad and naked women. Well, there we were, looking, laughing, and looking some more. We were totally absorbed and completely unaware that someone had moved up on us.

"Hello boys, nice evening isn't it?" There he was, halo and all, the Reverend Anthony Mattrazzo!

We stumbled with some stupid answer like, "Yes Father, it sure is." We were not sure what his next move might be but we were hoping he would not send us directly to hell!

To our surprise he simply said, "I need a couple of new altar boys so I would like for you two (me and Joey) to stop by the church tomorrow, after school, and we can discuss when you would like to begin your instruction." That was it . . . never said another word! He didn't even take the magazine! Later on though, we figured that one out. He didn't take the magazine because his partner, Father Negro, not speaking English, would not have been able to read the articles!

Joey and I were altar boys for the next five years and learned a lot from the Father just by being around him. He was a great asset to our church and a wonderful role model for the young people of the parish. Now, he's gone, Father Negro is gone, and so is the Sacred Heart Church. As they say: Gone but not forgotten.

SAINT DOMINIC?

UNCLE BABE & FRIEND

SACRED HEART CHURCH-MAHANOY CITY

FATHER NEGRO

AUNT MARY & HUSBAND CHICKIE
WISHER SACRED HEART CHURCH

AUNT MARY DI
LABIO & FRIEND

VIOLET CAPONE

COUSIN ALFIE
DI LABIO

DAD & UNCLE BABE WITH DRINKING
BUDDIES AT WITMER'S SALOON

UNCLE GLEN DUNNING AND DAD LIFTING A COOL ONE

PASTA, APRONS, AND BOXING

❖ ❖ ❖

"Feed a cold . . . feed a fever." That was my Mom's golden rule. She was always practicing the Italian tradition of "eat, eat, you'll feel better." In fact, she persistently practiced on both me and my sister. Whenever I brought a friend home she would say, "Sonny, your friend, he look-a skinny, ask if he wants something to eat." Nine times out of ten they'd say yes! No, she wasn't unique. The whole family was like that. For a few years we lived with my grandparents, Giuseppe (Joe) and Graziella (Grace) Di Labio, and wouldn't you know it, they liked to eat too. Not regular food mind you, but ITALIAN FOOD! Tons and tons of Italian food. There wasn't a (day go) by that the house didn't have that intoxicating aroma of freshly cooked marinara sauce. And to go with that, there was always meatballs, sweet sausage, and an assortment of pasta that would be the envy of any chef's menu. Home-made fettuccine, gnocchi, ravioli. You name it, they made it . . . and we ate it. Oh yea, and let us not forget grandmam's hot, Italian bread shouting out for some extra-virgin olive oil and Balsamic vinegar.

My favorite? Well, I had two of them. One being polenta, which was made from white cornmeal, smothered with marinara sauce, Romano cheese, and chunks of that sweet,Italian sausage. Polenta was pretty much a staple because it didn't cost very much to make and could feed an army . . . and we had the army! Dom De Luise once said he loved polenta because you could take the leftovers and use it as spackle to repair the cracks in your plaster. Then, whenever you got hungry, you could just lick the walls! But, my number one favorite of all time was, and still is, eggplant rolletine. Peel and slice the eggplant lengthwise, dredge the slices in flour, pass through a beaten egg bath, and fry until golden brown. Place one slab each of mozzarella and provolone cheese in the middle of each eggplant slice, add a healthy dollop of ricotta, some freshly chopped parsley, and a sprinkle of grated Romano. Roll up the stuffed eggplant slices and place them into a greased (olive oil) baking dish and top with a generous amount of marinara and grated Parmigiano Reggiano. Bake for 20 to 30 minutes at 350 degrees and mangia. My grandmam's specialty, now that was Italian!

My grandpap used to go into the hills, almost daily, to gather dandelions, mushrooms, and blueberries. They grew wild and were just there for the picking. He would usually take me and his dog, Blackie, along for company. But come to think of it, we were actually more than company. My grandmam sewed a few burlap sacks together and when we would get them filled, grandpap would drape a few over the dog's back, a couple on my back, and we would head for the house. Grandmam would empty the bags, wash the bounty, and soon we would be eating dandelion salads and blueberry pies. That, combined with what we got from the victory garden, was more than enough to feed us, as well as any visitors that might stop by.

When I arose in the mornings, first thing I usually saw was Mom and grandmam donning their aprons. And at bedtime . . . apron removal. Sometimes I wondered if they didn't have more aprons than dresses. They probably did. There were some Sundays though that we would go to Shenandoah for supper with the Polidore's. Now that was standing-room-only! My Dad's adopted family had twelve children by then(including him), and they all knew where that dining room table was. With Grandma Polidore's first six kids being girls, they easily slipped into the cooking routine and boy, did they have the aprons! For a family who were primarily coal miners, material things were a little hard to come by, but when it came to food, we were livin' on Wall Street. Sundays in Shenandoah also gave me a chance to mingle with my cousins, and believe me, there were many. We would compare notes, eat, eat some more, then we'd have dessert!

*   *   *   *   *

Back in Mahanoy City, me and grandpap loved to listen to that big radio console in the parlor. I think it was an RCA Victor. Great shows like Amos and Andy, Fibber McGee and Molly, Gang Busters, and Sam Spade. But most of all, he liked The Friday Night Fights. The broadcasts were usually from Madison Square Garden or the old Saint Nicholas Arena in New York City. I remember they were sponsored by Gillette Blue Blades, for that extra-smooth shave. On June 19, 1946, Joe Louis was to defend his World Heavyweight Title against Pittsburgh's Billy Conn for the second time, and it was to be aired from Yankee Stadium. Billy Conn almost dethroned Louis in their first match so me and grandpap were really excited about this one. Joe Louis was grandpap's favorite boxer and we were both eagerly awaiting the match. I don't remember what round, or any of the particulars, but with me and Blackie at his feet, grandpap took his final breath in his favorite chair. At first, I thought he was playing around, but when I got grandmam, I knew he was gone. Joe Louis won the fight, and I lost my grandpap. He was only 52. I was deeply saddened and had a hard time accepting his loss, but Blackie had it tougher. That poor dog stopped eating, and about eight days later, he was gone too.

Back in the old days, not many people could afford to have their loved ones laid out at the local funeral parlor; therefore, many of the deceased ended up in their own parlors. To a kid of about ten, that was creepy. Our parlor was crammed with an abundance of beautiful flowers, and bright lights to accentuate the open casket. I really had a hard time sleeping upstairs knowing that my grandpap was lying dead downstairs. Mom asked if I would like to see him and I remember replying with an emphatic no! To this day, I am so glad that no one forced me. Rest in peace, Grandpap Di Labio. I love you

DI GIAMARINO'S IN NEW
JERSEY. TIME TO EAT.

AUNT MARY DI MARINO & FRIENDS.
YES, IT'S TIME TO EAT AGAIN.

THE DI MARINO CLAN

SUNDAY DINNER AT GRANDMA
POLIDORE'S IN SHENANDOAH, PA.

MOM, PALMA, & AUNT STELLA
POLIDORE AT EAST END
PARK IN MAHANOY CITY

AUNT MARY DI MARINO

JOE LOUIS vs. BILLY CONN-JULY 19,1946 -
YANKEE STADIUM. THE NIGHT MY
GRANDPAP PASSED AWAY. (R.I.P)

GRANDPAP, GRANDMAM,
& AUNT MARY

DAD WITH ALL HIS BIOLOGICAL
SIBLINGS FROM JERSEY

WHY NOT... LET'S EAT AGAIN.

MINI-MAFIOSO

Everyone needs someone to blame, so I'm blaming the movies! Almost every Saturday, me and the boys were either at The Elks or The Vic watching the current gangster flicks starring James Cagney, Edward G. Robinson, or George Raft. And if it wasn't one of them, it was Leo Gorcey with The Dead End Kids, The East Side Kids, or The Bowery Boys. We would imitate them at play and soon we were imitating them in our daily lives. Years later, I actually met Leo Gorcey while I was working as a bar boy at Randall Race Track, just outside of Cleveland. My uncle, Frank Georgiana, got me the job there for the summer and made the introduction. I was star-struck!

I believe my first venture into thievery was the occasional heist of my Dad's cigarettes. He usually smoked Lucky Strikes and I figured . . . eh, if they were good enough for my old man, they were good enough for me. Now that's rationalization. The kids I hung around with did the same thing, so if one of us didn't score, the others could back it up. Eventually though, I streamlined my operation. Every other night or so, Mom would send me up to Peca's Company Store with a penciled list of stuff for Dad's lunch. Items such as: (5) slices of baloney, (2) apples, (2) TastyKakes, and (5) cigarettes.

Now Peca's also owned the coal mines where my Dad worked so there was no transaction of money, just "put it on the book." At the end of the week, whatever was owed was deducted from Dad's paycheck and everyone was happy. When Mom would give me the list, I would periodically change the number of cigarettes from 5 to 15, and I was happy too! In those days, you could buy cigarettes for a penny apiece and Mom and Dad never caught the drift. In fact, neither did anyone else. While other kids were picking up butts from the streets, me and my guys were livin' large.

One Saturday afternoon, me and Joey Faz decided we would like to have some ice cream from Kubert's Market. Unlike Peca's, it was new, spacious, well-lit, and surrounded with large, picture windows. Our parents rarely shopped there, so we surmised that no one would know us, and a heist would be easy. We agreed on Neapolitan ice cream sandwiches, two each, and we would slip them into the front of our pants. On our way out, we would buy a couple of Birch Beer sodas and have a little party over in the school yard. While slipping the ice cream sandwiches into our trousers, we were totally unaware that the store manager had the perfect view of a theft-in-progress. His highly polished security mirrors, which were suspended from the ceiling, left no doubt. He knew, and we didn't! Descending from his elevated catbird seat, he began to stalk us from aisle to aisle, but never stopped us to inquire. This goofy game began to take time and sure enough, time plus body heat began to equal . . . ice cream melting in pants! The situation became quite uncomfortable but what could we do, call a cop? Eventually, he made his way to the front of the store and waited for us to exit. We knew we were had and just wanted out. As we approached the front door he simply said, "If I ever see you two in my store again, I'll be speaking to your parents." That's it. No cops, no jail time, but the simple thought of me facing my old man kept me and Joey from that market for the duration. Have you ever had ice cream running down your legs before? Well, neither have I . . . not since that memorable day at Kubert's Market. As soon as we could find some privacy, we removed what was left from our pants and ran home in search of a bathroom. As I busted through my front door I heard Mom say, "Sonny, come here, I wanna talk to you." My frantic reply was, "Okay Ma, but I really gotta go to the bathroom . . . bad!"

While cleaning up, I began to laugh hysterically . . . Joey still had another block to run!

* * * * *

When I answered the door, I wasn't surprised to see Louie, but I was surprised to see the anxious look on his face.

"D.G., c'mon out," he said. "We gotta talk."

"Okay," I replied. "How about here on the porch."

"No, not here . . . I got some secret stuff we gotta talk about and we can't do it here.

Meet me in the school yard at six o'clock, okay?"

"All right, Louie, see you at six."

After supper, which I'm sure was some sort of pasta, Mom gave me her list for Peca's and reminded me not to forget. Old Pops could get a little upset whenever I forgot the stuff for his lunch. It was about 5:30, so that would give me enough time to get (our) cigarettes and meet Louie by six. I entered the school yard and heard Louie.

"Eh, D.G., over here." As we sat on the concrete steps, Louie blurted out, "I went to Newberry's today and stole sumthin'."

"Great," I said. "What did you steal?"

He opened up his hand and said, "Dis!"

It was a key! Just a regular, old house key!

"So what's the big deal?" I said.

"Well, dis ain't no regular, old house key," he responded. "Dis is a skeleton key!

It said so right on the tag."

I never claimed to be the brightest bulb in the circuit, but this was passing me by.

"Louie, what in the hell are you talking about?"

39

"Dis key opened up my front door, and I want you to try it on yours, but don't let anyone see you. Cause look, if it works there too, maybe we could find a store or business to knock off."

Now it started to come together.

"Okay, Lou, gimme the key, and I'll get back to you as soon as I try it."

We went our separate ways, and I couldn't wait to try the key. When I got to my house, I checked to see if anyone was in the parlor or could actually see the front door. Luckily, there was no one around. Mom and grandmam were upstairs with my sister and my Dad and Uncle Babe were already at Adukaitis. I quietly slipped the key into the lock, gave it a turn to the left, and son-of-a-bitch . . . it actually worked! Mamma—mia, I couldn't believe it! A skeleton key from the five and dime! As I was retrieving the key from the lock, Mom yelled, "Sonny . . . what are you doing at the front door?"

"Nuthin' Ma, the door knob was a little stuck." I swear, that lady had eyes in the back of her head!

The following day, I gave Louie the results, and the wheels began to turn. First thing we agreed on was secrecy. No one would know about this key except me and Louie. Remember, this was the era of "Loose Lips Sink Big Ships." It was also the era and area of minimal crime. There was no need for dead-bolt locks and bars on the windows. In fact, my Uncle Babe had a '38 Buick convertible that sat in front of our house with the top down and a "toggle" switch to turn over the engine. No keys required. Believe me, this was a different time, and the perfect time for me and Louie to make the big score.

On the corner of East 13th and Mahanoy Street, there was Price's Potato Chips and Pretzels. No production going on, just a large warehouse. After much deliberation, we chose the warehouse as a potential target. It was just a two-man operation, and each evening they would close by dark. They had a couple of panel trucks and would deliver large, circular tins of potato chips and pretzels to beer joints, church bazaars, and individual residents. I remember Mom buying a can or two. One night, we decided to try "the key" in a side door, and I'll be damned if it didn't work there too! This was beginning to get exciting! The only problem we could foresee was the location. The target was half-a-block from Louie's house and directly across the street from a poker club called, "The Bucket of Blood," where most of our dads hung out. The stage was set . . . if we had the balls!

After staking out the place for a few weeks, we noticed that Wednesday nights seemed to be our best bet. For some reason, there were fewer guys at "The Bucket," and the two guys that worked at Price's usually left a little early. We planned a dry run to locate the cache, check the time element, and establish an escape route . . . just like in the movies. Everything went smooth and we were on! Oh yea, we also took the *Oath Of Omerta:* The Mafia's Code of Honor and Silence. This was our business, and ours alone. In other words . . . *we don't know nuthin'—didn't see nuthin—and we wasn't even dere!*

On a warm summer's evening in 1948, me and Louie, both dressed in black, met at the 12th Street School yard to nail down our final thoughts. This was it, Wednesday night, the big event. Louie was going in, and I would be the look out. If anyone came by, I would throw a small rock at the metal siding of the warehouse and walk away while Louie would douse the flashlight and freeze. When the coast was clear, I would return, knock three times on the door, and we would resume the caper. Louie was to take one can each of pretzels and potato chips, place them into a black, cloth bag and exit the warehouse. I would lock the door and we would head for the hills.

It went without a hitch! No one came by and there was hardly anyone at the poker club. Prior to the heist, we dug a hole at one of our favorite hill hideouts. Kinda like our own little fort. We lined the hole with cardboard and fashioned a false top to make it look like the surroundings. You know, like camouflage. The cans fit perfectly, and me, Louie, and the guys now had potato chips and pretzels to go with our ice cream and sodas. We hit Price's about four times that summer, and then we let it go. We were hoping to see something in the local newspaper but I guess we didn't make a large enough dent in their inventory. The story never made it to print, Louie retired "the key," and to this day, we will both contend, *"We don't know nuthin' – didn't see nuthin' – and we wasn't even dere!"*

In the fall of 1949, there was an unbelievable event that took place in Mahanoy City. A few black limos, bearing license plates from New York and New Jersey, found their way into our little community. Exiting those limos were small groups of men wearing expensive suits, tailored topcoats, and fancy fedoras. They zeroed in on a house near the corner of East 8th and Mahanoy Street. Donny Heckler, said, "It must be a funeral, or somethin'." I had other thoughts. We rounded up some of the boys, settled across the street, and watched. Finally, the light went on . . . Mafia meeting! Our little coal mining town was hosting a Mafia meeting! We had a Police Chief and two patrolmen but none were on duty that particular weekend. Hmmm . . . go figure. The meeting lasted for two days and not a shot was fired. That was good. All the shades were pulled and we couldn't see very much, but eventually, we found out it was nothing more than a heavy-duty poker game! Yea, right. On Sunday evening, one by one, the limos loaded up and headed out. The meeting (game) was over. It took me until 1972 to figure out whether Vito Corleone could have visited our fair city!

EDWARD G. ROBINSON

"THE KEY"

GEORGE RAFT

LEO GORCEY

JAMES CAGNEY

SURROGATE DADDY

It's very important that you don't get me wrong here. My Dad was the best dad a kid could ask for, but he definitely lacked the sports gene. Any other subject of life and he was there. Uncle Babe however, was a bona-fide, class A, multi-sport aficionado who knew it all, and took the time to teach it to me. Baseball, basketball, football, you name it, and he was the bible. If I had to pick a sport that possibly interested my Dad, it would probably be boxing. He got most of his training at Adukaiti's Tavern, and I must admit, he was quite good at it.

When Babe, my Mom's youngest brother, returned from the war, he kinda took me under his wing and taught me about sports in general, and baseball in particular. Shortly after his discharge, he went to work for Kaier's Brewery and soon became their third baseman. Kaiers was in a local Industrial Baseball League and played most of their games within a fifty mile radius so, I got to see many. I don't remember what the winner's trophy looked like, but I'm sure it resembled a keg!

Me and "The Babe" spent many an hour up at the old East End Park . . . hitting, pitching, shagging fly balls, and counting the bounces on grounders. Over and over, again and again. I did it until I got it right, and I loved it! He bought me my first glove, and thanks to him, I eventually turned out to be a pretty good shortstop/pitcher, with a consistent batting average around .300. Oh yea, and after each session we would stop at George's Ice Cream Parlor for a strawberry shake. Hmmm, was it the baseball or the shake? Little did I know, that many years later, I would be doing the same for my sons that Babe was doing for me.

Believe it or not, he also got me into scrap booking! Nothing like it is today, but we used to cut out the sports action photos from the local Record American and thePhiladelphia Inquirer and paste them into categorized binders. Hockey, boxing, baseball . . . the whole works. Sundays were great . . . many, many black and white photos for the taking. What I would give to have those books today.

Between Dad and Babe, it didn't take me very long to learn how to drive. I had a 1930 Model A Ford and a 1938 Buick convertible at my disposal, and by the time I was twelve, I could handle both of them. That Model A was something special though. One night I remember Dad coming home "a little loaded" and Mom asking as to how he was able to drive. Through a silly grin he replied, "Genny, the car knows the way." It took Mom a little while.

Hunting and fishing. Man, those were some great times. Babe belonged to the Mahanoy City Rod and Gun Club, and he loved the great outdoors just as much as he enjoyed competitive sports. We used to go down to Lakewood, a local amusement park, and practically spend the whole day on a row boat catching "blue gills." They looked like over-sized gold fish and were great fun to reel in. Babe would throw back everything we caught, except for the rainbow trout, which were his favorites. We usually had a small ice chest with baloney sandwiches, a couple of sodas, and enough Kaier's beer to keep Babe afloat. By following his lead, I eventually figured out that it was okay to work and play hard, but it was equally as important to relax as well. I was a little too young for the hunting trips but occasionally, I did get to go on some rabbit and squirrel expeditions. During the deer hunting season, Babe would head up to the Pocono Mountains and when he was due home, I would sit on the front porch and watch for the Buick to come whipping around the corner with a big, old buck strapped to the fender. And believe me, it happened more often than not.

* * * * *

Prior to going to Europe, Babe was stationed at Fort Sam Houston near San Antonio, Texas, and he sent me one of the best presents I ever got in my life. A pair of leather cowboy boots! I couldn't believe it when Mom yelled, "Sonny, hurry, Babe sent you a package from Texas!" They were a little big, but who cared. Wore those babies 'til they fell apart. The Babe was a sergeant in the U.S. Army, 2nd Infantry Division, and during the war, I was always looking in the newspapers and watching newsreels to see where his unit was. At night, I used to pray that he was well and would return safely. Especially after he sent me those boots!

Dad never made it to the military because, during the war years, being a coal miner with a couple of kids was an automatic deferment. They needed the coal, to make the steel, to manufacture the tanks, planes, and ships that were mandated by the U.S. Government. Besides, who would keep that bar stool warm at Adukaiti's! Just kidding, Pop.

A few years ago, Babe sent me another package. A piece of anthracite coal, a brick from the demolished 12th Street School, and an old photo of him in uniform. A short note was enclosed and read, *"To my first nephew, who I saw, and still see, as a sweet little boy with leather boots from Texas. Remember me always . . . Uncle Babe."*

Shortly afterward, the Babe passed away. But he can rest assured that he will always be with me. To him, I simply say, "Thanks for the greatest of memories and above all, thanks for being my surrogate daddy."

GRANDMAM DI LABIO & SON - UNCLE BABE

UNCLE BABE -
U.S. ARMY

UNCLE BABE -
THE ALAMO

UNCLES - ERNIE &
BABE DI LABIO

THE BABE IN
EUROPE

BABE IN TEXAS

SGT. BABE DI LABIO
AND FRIEND

UNCLE BABE & PALMA

"THE BABE"

THE EAST END

For my first fourteen years we lived on the east side of town. Ten years on South Street with my grandparents, Graziella and Giuseppe, and after grandpap passed . . . about four years with Uncle Babe on Pine Street. His was a large, row house, many bedrooms, and within close range of 12th Street School and my friends. There was me, my sister, Mom and Dad, grandmam, and Babe. Sounds like a crowd, but in those days, multi-family households were the norm. My Dad was working the mines, Babe had a job at the brewery, and I don't remember any major problems. Besides, Dad and Babe were "drinking buddies" so I don't think they could have asked for a better deal.

About a block away from the house was one of the best places in the whole, wide world. The East End Park! Baseball fields, running track, football field, and basketball courts. Swing sets, monkey bars, and see-saws. Picnic tables, fire pits, and barbeques were everywhere. Once a year, the circus would come to town and us kids would help them set up for free tickets. I'm talking about the "Big Top" folks! Real live tigers, trapeze artists, clowns, jugglers, elephants, and pretty women who rode fancy white horses. The Midway was loaded with weird acts like the sword swallower, the fire eater, tattoo man, and the snake lady. Ringling Brothers would come in by truck and train and make their way up Centre Street to the East End Park. Fire trucks, the MCHS band, and the red, white, and blue were the order of the day. Now that was a parade! It used to leave me breathless. So did some of the shows that we got to see, that we weren't supposed to see! We were livin' in a world that sadly, no longer exists.

Guess who got to play on that manicured baseball field at the park? No, not me . . . it was the Mahanoy City Brewers, a minor league ball club that was affiliated with the New York Yankees and played on most summer weekends. They were in the North Atlantic League and faced other minor league teams such as: The Carbondale Pioneers, The Kingston Dodgers, and The Nazareth Barons. I remember one Sunday, the Washington Pilots (from the American Negro League) came into town for an exhibition game and totally dismantled us. These guys were good! So good, I don't think we ever asked them back. Tony Ciori was our centerfielder and he could not have been much more than 5'-5" tall, but boy, could he spray that ball around the field. Every time he came to the plate, the crowd would chant, "Push 'em up, Tony!" . . . and he usually did. When we played the Pilots, Tony got a couple of singles, and I still have this vision of him, standing next to their first baseman, who looked to be about seven feet tall! We used to hang around both dugouts just waiting for someone to break a bat or throw us an old ball. Our dads would take the broken wooden bats, nail them up, tape them, and we were ready to go. Nothing too good for the sandlot boys. Recently, while browsing a local sporting goods store, I noticed an aluminum Little League bat for about $250! Yes Virginia, times have really changed.

Somehow, with all of the major events that took place at the East End Park, we always seemed to get in free. No, we didn't have season passes, we just knew where all the fence holes were. Mr. Pollack, the park manager, would patch up one entry, and we would create two more. We would go over, under, or through whatever he had built. I'm sure the old man often dreamt about us at night. One evening, me and a bunch of the guys, broke into the park just to chase each other in the dark and have some fun. We noticed a diffused light coming from the equipment shack which was located just beyond the home-run fence in left field. We decided to check it out thinking that maybe someone just forgot to turn out the lights. But then again, knowing Mr. Pollack, that was highly unlikely. As we got closer to the shack, we heard a lot of giggling and laughter, and the anticipation began to build. We peered into the dimly lit room through a dirty, glass pane, and could not believe our eyes! There were three guys and three girls, all high school age, in various stages of nakedness . . . playing strip poker! One of them was Donny Heckler's older brother, and Donny was busting a gut. In fact, we all were. We watched for a few minutes but then decided we had better hit the road before they caught us. We loudly rapped on the window, disappeared into the darkness, and I remember thinking, *Man, I can't wait 'til I get into high school!*

In the autumn of the year, Friday nights and the East End Park were reserved for Coach Joe Pilconis and high school football. And, if I'm not mistaken, we played in the Black Diamond League. Believe me, this was serious business. We played other coal mining towns in the area, and each one thought they were better than the next. Minersville, Mount Carmel, Ashland, St. Clair, Summit Hill, Shamokin, Tamaqua, and especially Shenandoah. The Mahanoy City Maroons vs. the Shenandoah Blue Devils. It was a rivalry no less significant than the Cleveland Browns and the Pittsburgh Steelers. This was smash-mouth football at its finest . . . both on the field and in the stands. Again, we did not need any tickets. How about that!

Norm Jones was the baseball coach at Mahanoy City High and was very instrumental in getting us younger kids a ball field up at the East End Park. There was no grass in the infield and come to think of it, not very much in the outfield either.

Mr. Jones created a Sandlot League for us, and we had a great time learning the game. I got to use those basic skills "The Babe" taught me, and in turn, passed them on to my peers. This was not your organized, "Little League" baseball of today, but simply, an unorganized bunch of kids with very little adult participation, and you know what . . . we liked it that way. We played to win and had fun doing it! Nowadays, I'm not sure of either. With our broken bats and beat-up balls, we were both grateful and appreciative. I played for a couple of local sponsors, *King's Cleaners and Klipola's Sporting Goods,* and they really treated us good. Occasionally, they would even spring for ice cream and soda. We pranced around town wearing their monogrammed tee-shirts and ball caps like we were part owners of the companies! Ours was a simple, but enjoyable life back then, and the sandlot field gave us yet, another reason to head for the East End Park.

In the 1300 block of East Pine Street, behind Kerry Richards' house, we had an old rim and backboard mounted on a street light pole. Our own personal basketball court to be used day or night. We played H-O-R-S-E until it was coming out of our ears. Many a night you could hear the neighborhood mothers shouting for their boys, ala the Henry Aldridge show. We didn't have Play Stations or X-Boxes, no video games or movie discs, smart phones or personal computers. We just had friends, and we found them outside . . . every day and every night . . . playing games. Today, the East End Park is a third-world shadow of what it used to be . . . but the memory lingers on.

DAD, MOM, & PALMA

MOM, DAD, & ME

DAD, MOM, GRANDMAM, & ME

AUNT ANNIE
& GUIDO
DELLA
ROCCA

MOM, DAD, ME & FRIENDS

THE CAPONE
SISTERS

ME, MOM
& DOGS

JEANETTE
CAPONE & PALMA

MOM, VIOLET
& PALMA

PALMA & VIOLET CAPONE   GENO CAPONE

SPRINGTIME AND SUMMER

❖ ❖ ❖

Frank Sinatra, Jack Palance, and Doris Day. Glenn Miller, the Dorsey Brothers, Louie Armstrong, and Vaughn Monroe. Hollywood, you say? Nope, it was Lakewood . . . a few short miles from Mahanoy City, and better known as "The Lake." An amusement park primarily designed for coal miners and their families, in a long-gone era before television and air conditioners. A place to cool off and relax. A place to dance, swim, roller skate, go canoeing, take a ride in a motor boat, do a little fishing, ride the "flying horses" (carousel), and have ethnic family picnics. Many of the miners were from Eastern Europe and on any given Sunday you would be subjected to the delightful scent of foreign foods from Poland, Hungary, Lithuania, and the Czech Republic. Or maybe the addictive aroma of large containers of Italian marinara sauce, bubbling over an open flame, while awaiting the ultimate pasta connection.

I lived about four miles from paradise and I loved it. What a wonderful place to spend a childhood. During springtime and summer, me and the guys spent a lot of time down at "The Lake" and it never cost us a dime to get there, or back. We just threw out our thumbs and we were on our way. I wouldn't recommend hitch-hiking today, but back then, it worked for us.

58

One of my favorite places was the gigantic swimming pool, occasionally visited by Buster Crabb (Tarzan). There was a large, free-standing platform in the water with about a 30 foot high diving tower near the edge. I remember me and the boys climbing that tower one day, but we all chickened-out . . . well, all except for one . . . Donny (Superman) Heckler . . . he took the plunge. It's been said that Donny had more courage than brains. Maybe he did, but that's why we loved him.

* * * * *

Springtime and summer also meant Camden, N.J. That's where all of my Dad's biological siblings resided and I used to look forward to those two hour train trips. Loved that dining car! But especially loved those major league baseball games at Shibe Park in Philadelphia. If my memory serves me correctly, the Philadelphia Athletics (American League) and the Philadelphia Phillies (National League) both played at Shibe Park so I had the best of both worlds. My Uncle Tony, married to my Dad's sister Katy, was a baseball fanatic and on most visits to Camden, we automatically took in a ball game. My uncle would jam five or six kids (all cousins) into his old car and we would head across the Delaware River to see the likes of Joe DiMaggio, Phil Rizzuto or Ted Williams. On any other day we could be watching StanMusial, Robin Roberts, and Richie Ashburn. I even got to see Ron Northey play! What an honor it was to see "these guys" do their thing.

You're probably thinking my Uncle Tony must have had big bucks in order to continually take a bunch of kids to a bevy of major league baseball games. Well, that ain't necessarily so. In and around 1948, prices were quite reasonable. For example: Cost of "bleacher seats" . . . 50 to 75 cents, hot dog . . . 25 cents, soft drink . . . 10 cents, and average gas prices were about 15 cents a gallon. Ah yes, the good old days!

My dad's two brothers, Frank and Jimmy, both worked many years for Campbell's Soup right there in Camden and I used to love to go to their houses. Uncle Frank was musically inclined and played the saxophone. His daughter Claudette, played piano, and his son Frankie, played the accordion. Uncle Frank and Aunt Louise lived across the street from Dudley Park and that's where me and my cousins spent most of our time. It seemed like every town I went to I had cousins! Uncle Jimmy was a great guy as well. He and his wife Connie, had a little girl named Marian who wasn't born until 1947, so we didn't get to hang out very much. But, getting back to her dad Jimmy, well this is weird. My Dad, Eddie, and his brother Jimmy, looked so much alike they could have been twins! They even sounded alike! Now here's the rub. My Dad's birth certificate shows that he was born in December, 1915 and Uncle Jimmy's says he was born in January, 1916! Is that reproductively possible? Always was a mystery and I guess it always will be.

Dad's two sisters, Katy and Lena, were great people too. Katy and her husband Tony (the baseball guy), had two sons, Junior and Joey. Lena and her husband Barney, also had two sons, Dominic and Tommy. Side trips to Atlantic City and Wildwood were always exciting. I remember the Boardwalk and seeing Billy Eckstine, the old jazz/pop singer, at the Steel Pier. Eventually, we would all meet at Uncle Frank's house and it was good food, good music, and park time with the cousins.

Another occasional stop in Camden was my great-uncle Joe's house. He had fig trees and grape vines growing everywhere and a large, covered table for eating outside. His back yard had the look of an Italian mini-vineyard. There was definitely a touch of Italy in Camden, N.J. Uncle Joe used to make home-made wine for the Jersey family and I think he really loved his job. I think I loved his job too, because every time we would visit, Uncle Joe would offer me and the cousins a shot glass of his home-made (dago red) wine! My Mom was not too happy about this so I would always look to my Dad for his approval, and he never turned me down. Like I said before, if it's good enough for my old man, it was good enough for me.

* * * * *

Speaking of the famiglia, let me give you the run down on the Di Labio's. Uncle Tony (Antonio), the oldest son of Giuseppe and Graziella, was born in Italy. He and his wife,Maria, had eight children: Guido, Camillo, Nicola, Carmela, Graziella, Laura, Gabriella, and Rita. Aunt Mary, also born in Italy, was married to a guy named Chickie Wisher and did not have any off-spring. I remember they were married at my old alma mater, the Sacred Heart Church. Aunt Annie married Glenwood Dunning and had two children: Louis and Grace and they resided in Pottstown, Pennsylvania. Next was my Mom, Genevieve, and then came Uncle Ernie. Ernie was married to Dorothy and she hailed from Shenandoah. They had two kids: Little Ernie and Grace. Last, but not least . . . my Uncle Babe. He married Elvira Marina and had one child named Alfie. Elvira also had a brother, Rupe Marina, who was very instrumental in getting me a butt-whipping that I would never forget. I'll discuss that situation in the next few pages.

Uncle Tony, and his wife Maria, came to North America in the 1960s and settled his family in Ottawa, Canada. What's a little unusual about Uncle Tony's story, was the fact that when his parents, Giuseppe and Graziella, migrated to America . . . they left him in Italy! Baby Antonio was just two years old and the plan was for him to stay with his maternal grandmother, (the Garofalos), until he was old enough to travel to America and re-join the rest of his family. Sadly . . . that never happened. I'm sure that must have played heavily on my Grandmam Di Labio's heart strings as she went through life not really knowing, or interacting with, her eldest son and those eight grandkids.

But wait . . . the Di Labio dilemma continues. When my Uncle Ernie returned from the war he seemed very anxious and unsettled. It was probably the equivalent of todays PTSD (posttraumatic stress disorder). Back then they called it shell-shock and/or battle fatigue. Rumor was that Ernie saw more than his share of battlefield action and it evidently had taken its toll. A few months after his return . . . he disappeared! To my knowledge, no one in the family ever heard from, or seen him again. That is until a few years ago when my Aunt Elvira received a letter from a gentleman, somewhere in Wisconsin, stating that Ernie had passed away and that he and his brother called my Uncle Ernie . . . Dad! According to this young man's recollection, Uncle Ernie met and married their mother, many years ago in Chicago, moved to Wisconsin, fathered and raised these two sons, and lived happily ever after. That's the last I ever heard of this story, but to my Grandmam Di Labio, I must say . . . God bless you, for yours was a rough road to travel.

* * * * *

When I was about to turn seven years of age, my Mom threw me a birthday party . . . and no one came! No one except the man from the Board of Health who put a bright red placard on my front door which read: SCARLET FEVER—Do Not Enter! Man, that was terrible. You must remember, at seven years of age my whole life was outside . . . running, jumping, and laughing. Now I was quarantined for 30 days and could do nothing more than look out my bedroom window! I often wonder whether the kids of today could have handled that . . . without electronics.

Our family doctor was a great guy by the name of Mark Holland. I remember him as a young, intelligent sort who seemed to like kids, and hardly ever took money for services rendered. During my 30 day quarantine he would drop by the house every two or three days, check me out, and Mom would talk him into some pasta or dessert. In fact, he came by for my birthday party when no one else did. We had chocolate cake, vanilla ice cream, and coffee. Yes, coffee! Chase & Sanborn coffee! Back in those days, a lot of children drank the brew with a little touch of good, old Carnation Evaporated Milk. I guess it kind of gave us that "adult feeling."

One night, while still under quarantine, I started having hallucinations. To compound the event, I could hear the eerie train whistles as they pierced the silence of the valley, and honest to God, they sounded like they were right in my room. It all eventually passed but that night I really thought I was going to buy the farm. Sixty-seven years later I experienced the same hallucinations (dancing flowers on the wall) while in the hospital having my aortic valve replaced. The cardiac surgeon said the damaged valve could have been caused by the scarlet fever! Small world.

As time progressed, the quarantine was lifted and I was eager to re-join the gang. Doc Holland gave me a clean bill of health but cautioned me to go easy for a while. Naturally, I was in a hurry. My first night back on the streets, me and the guys were in the 12th Street School yard playing "Tag." I just happened to be "it" and was searching, in the dark, for someone to tag. I thought I saw Joey Fazio going into the school yard trash shed; I followed and someone pushed me from behind. I went ass over tea kettle and upon exit, it felt like my left hand was wet. I soon located some light and sure enough, my left hand was wet . . . with blood! My middle finger was hanging on by the skin and Pauley Phillips (the one who pushed me) took me across the street to his house while Joey ran to get my Mom, who in turn, had to get my Dad from Adukaiti's, to get me to Doc Holland's. As he was sewing up my hand he said, "Sonny, I told you to slow down and if you don't, I'll put you back under quarantine!" I thought to myself, *"He can't do that . . . can he?"* My Dad laughed and told the Doc, "Good idea." This time I followed the doctor's orders and sure enough, my hand healed nicely and I slowly regained my strength.

* * * * *

One afternoon, me and the boys were hanging around the Train Station, playing on the luggage carts and waiting for a passenger train so we could check out the people. It doesn't sound like much, but it made our day. Donny was sitting on one of the carts wearing that cerebral look.

"Hey, let's go swimming," he said.

We all replied, "Okay, let's take the next freight."

"Wait," Donny said. "I can't go . . . I don't have a bathing suit!"

We totally cracked up. Everybody in the world knew that bathing suits were not required at the abandoned mine swimming hole! The innocence was golden.

The plan was simple. We would hop a freight to the Tamaqua tunnel, jump off there, enter the tunnel and wait for another train to come by and scare the hell out of us! If you've never done it . . . don't! Believe me, the excitement level of hugging the inside of a tunnel while a train passes through, could give you cause to wet your pants! It was taking too long waiting on that second train so, we decided to walk the tracks for the remainder of the way. Our swimming hole had that cool, clear water and the weather was perfect . . . hot and humid. We were surrounded by rolling hills of green for as far as the eye could see. Bull frogs, tad poles, and towards evening . . . lightning bugs. As I look back, it reminds me of the adventures of Tom Sawyer and Huckleberry Finn. We hopped another freight home and we were ready to fight another day.

Springtime and summer, and the clothes were always hanging on the line. The line was a "pulley line" that went from our back porch to a post in our back yard. You washed clothes on Monday, took them out to the porch, clothes-pinned them to the line, and sent them flapping into the wind. All of your unmentionables were exposed to the world! But, so were your neighbor's, and their neighbor's too. I remember when

Mom got her first washing machine. I believe it was a Maytag (ringer type), and she was ecstatic! If Dad would have given her a choice between that washing machine or a ten carat diamond . . . I know she would have chosen the washer! The difficult part about drying your wash on the line, by way of the elements, was sometimes your "whites" dried to a darker shade of gray than when you first put them out! The culprit was the daily coal dust floating through the valley, but what the hell, they were the exact same shade as the ladies' next door.

*   *   *   *   *

And then there was Rupe Marina. Rupe was a couple of years older than me and his mom and dad owned Marina's Saloon which was located just north of my house. Rupe was a tough kid, a hard worker, and always had money in his pocket. Occasionally, he would hang around with us guys but most of the time he had to work at the beer joint.

I remember one day, Rupe and Louie Fazio were playing in Rupe's backyard and there was an explosion! They had a couple of carbide lanterns, some canned calcium carbide, and they were trying to re-fuel the lamps. They somehow got a little water in the carbide can which created a combustible and explosive gas and Rupe struck a match to shed some light on the situation. Indeed he did! During the explosion, they suffered from minor facial burns, but were considered lucky. Never a dull moment.

I also remember a Friday evening, while on my way to find the gang, Rupe asked where I was headed. After my response, he stated the boys were probably down on Market Street at the "Shooting Gallery." I agreed but mentioned that I didn't have very much money to which he replied, "Don't worry about it . . . I'm loaded." We got there about 7:00 PM and the place was jumping. And sure enough, the Fazio brothers and Donny Heckler were also in attendance. For hours and hours we shot pellet guns and played carnival games trying to win kewpie dolls and other prizes, but I think the odds were stacked against us. Before we knew it, time slipped by and it was about 10:00 PM. The guys said they were heading home but Rupe talked me into staying a little longer. After all, I was having a great time . . . so why not? We got totally into the excitement and time was not a factor.

Actually, time was not a factor until about midnight. That's when I noticed my Dad and one of his drinking buddies, Monk Kubilis, walking into the "Gallery!" Dad grabbed me by the back of my neck and we began the "March To Bataan!" Upon my exit, I looked around for Rupe, but he had luckily disappeared. While dragging me along, Dad asked if I was aware that Mom had called the cops because she was worried sick? Before I could answer he cuffed me behind the ear and then I knew I was in big trouble.

While heading for the house, we passed by Adukaiti's and Monk told my Dad he would see him later. I was hoping Dad would send me home, follow Monk's lead, and we could talk about this in the morning . . . but no such luck. We busted through the front door and Dad headed for his bedroom. Within seconds, his 200 pound frame was standing in the parlor holding his truck driver's belt, better known as the "strap." He would wear this four inch wide belt whenever he had to drive one of the big coal trucks down at the mine, but tonight it would be used in a different manner! Being a southpaw, he grabbed me by the upper right arm and began to whip my butt like I've never been whipped before. My little sister was crying and my Mom was screaming, "Eddie, Eddie . . . stop it, that's enough!" For an eleven year old kid, I assumed I took the beating pretty well, or so I thought. The next few days the pain was excruciating!

I had welts on top of my welts and found myself standing to eat my meals. That was my first whippin' and believe me, it was going to be my last.

You know, not one time during that whippin' did my Dad say, "This is going to hurt me more than it is you!" I guess that only happens in the movies. The following morning Rupe came by to see if I had survived and before leaving, he asked if I wanted to go down to the "Shooting Gallery!"

*   *   *   *   *

Springtime and summer. A special time for young kids back then. The school year was coming to an end and we all looked forward to that summer vacation. It would give us far more time for running, jumping, laughing, and "street games." Kick-the-Can, Jack Dempsey, Hide-and-Seek, and Red Rover. Maybe a little Dodge-Ball, Hot-Potato, Tag, or Stick Ball. We loved Cracker Jacks and prizes, Ice Pops with (2) sticks to share with a friend, catching "lightning bugs" in a jar, and climbing trees. How about see-saws and swings, jumping on the bed, and playing Cowboys and Indians, especially after watching Hopalong Cassidy in a western, at the Victoria Theatre.

Kool-Aid was the drink of summer and an occasional swig from a garden hose could hit the spot as well. What could be better than giving a buddy a ride on the handle bars of your bike while listening to the sound of your baseball cards smacking against the spokes of your tires? Most major decisions were made by "eeny-meeny-miney-mo" and when we discussed the subject of race . . . we were talking of who could run the fastest! What a joy it was to have three or four best friends, instead of one. Friends that would spin 'round and 'round, get dizzy, and fall down in uncontrollable laughter . . . with no drugs required. The word boredom was definitely not in our vocabulary.

GRANDMAM &
ELVIRA DI LABIO

UNCLE FRANK DI GIAMARINO

"THE ANDREWSKI
SISTERS"

IT'S TIME TO EAT AGAIN

UNCLE
ERNIE DI
LABIO

UNCLES BARNEY &
FRANK W/ GRANDPA
POLIDORE & DAD

UNCLE ERNIE DI LABIO

DAD'S UNCLE-MIKE PILLO &
FAMILY BROCKTON, PA.

MOM'S FIRST
WASHING
MACHINE

AUNT LOUISE, UNCLE FRANK & CLAUDETTE
DI GIAMARINO-ATLANTIC CITY, N. J.

CLAUDETTE, AUNT LOUISE,
& FRANKIE-DUDLEY PARK

UNCLE JIMMY
DI GIAMARINO
DAD'S TWIN?

AUNT LENA DI GIAMARINO

AUNT LENA &
UNCLE BARNEY

ME & COUSIN
DOMINIC - LAKEWOOD

MOM, AUNT LENA, AUNT KATY,
& GRANDMA POLIDORE

ME, PALMA, & MOM

UNCLE FRANK & AUNT LOUISE - WEDDING

FRANKIE, AUNT LOUISE, &
CLAUDETTE CAMDEN, N.J.

COUSIN
DOMINIC-CAMDEN

UNCLE FRANK, AUNT LENA, AUNT KATY, & DAD

UNCLE BARNEY & DAD

COUSIN DOMINIC & ME

LAKEWOOD PARK

UNCLE BARNEY, AUNT LENA, MOM,
DAD, PALMA, TOMMY, & ME

UNCLE BABE, GRANDMAM,
& UNCLE TONY

UNCLE ERNIE

COUSINS GRACE & LOUIS -
CHILDREN OF AUNT ANNIE
& GLEN DUNNING

AUTUMN AND WINTER

◇◇◇ ❖ ❖❖ ◇◇◇

The changing of the leaves . . . what a spectacular event! Every year, around late September, millions of leaves surrounding the borough would change from a rich, forest green to a galaxy of yellow, orange, brown and red. A beautiful transition that no mere mortal could ever attain. The scene was unbelievable as we would walk through that festival of color to hook a few catties (catfish) at the East End fishing hole. Those autumn leaves would also remind us that the World Series was just around the corner.

The Fall Classic of 1948 was to feature the Cleveland Indians vs. the Boston Braves. Many believed that pitching would be the dominant factor and right they were. Cleveland's pitching staff was led by Bob Feller, Bob Lemon, and Gene Bearden while the Braves countered with Johnny Sain and Warren Spahn. Cleveland's Larry Doby (first black to play in the American League) would hit .318 for the Series while first baseman, Earl Torgeson would hit .389 for the Braves. Being a shortstop myself, you must know that Cleveland's Lou Boudreau was one of my favorites. The Indians took the World Series, 4 games to 2, and to this date, have never won another! To the best of my knowledge, none of these guys were ever signed to anything but single-year contracts and in 1948, as the American League MVP, Bob Feller's salary was about

$40,000. In 1950, a year after his worst major league season, Feller went to then General Manager Hank Greenberg, and asked for a 25% pay cut . . . and got it! Who could you name that would do that today? Little did I know, that a few years later, the Cleveland Indians would be my home-town team.

To me, autumn was also the perfect time of year for "doggie frizzles and roasted mickeys." You might ask, "What the hell is that?" Well, it's really nothing more than good old hot dogs and baked, russet potatoes! Again, at the East End Park, we had a number of open fire pits at our disposal and we used them quite often. All we needed were some hot dogs and buns, mustard and catsup, russet potatoes, a few wire hangers, a couple bottles of soda, some matches . . . and the party was on. We didn't even have to wrap the potatoes in tin foil. Just throw them into the fire and retrieve them when they were totally black on the outside and delectably soft on the inside. A little salt and butter would complete the process. As a hobo might say, "Nothing fancy here. No chromium grilles or flo-metered propane tanks. Nothing but the sweet life, at its lowest common denominator."

Peca's Coal Company had one of the first "black and white" TV sets in the area and they were always kind enough to let us kids come up to their company office to watch the Army/Navy football game being broadcast from Philadelphia. Army fullback, Doc Blanchard and halfback, Glenn Davis were known as "Mr. Inside and Mr. Outside" and they were phenomenal. All us kids idolized them. Blanchard won the Heisman Trophy in 1945, and his pal, Davis won it in 1946. Glenn Davis went to Bonita High School in La Verne, California and I understand his He is man is proudly on display in their trophy case. Nice gesture. I can't tell you how many times me and the guys raced up and down that football field at the East End Park pretending to be Glenn Davis or Doc Blanchard . . . straight-arming and hurdling imaginary tacklers on our way to that illusionary, game-winning touchdown. Now that, my friends, was the real definition of "fantasy football!"

And let us not forget, coal miners hockey on the creek. Goulashes instead of skates, a small piece of coal as the puck, and some dead branches pulled from a nearby tree. The Market Street Creek was frozen over and the stage was set for Gordie Howe. Hockey was not one of our long-suites, but everyone knew of the great professional,Gordie Howe and we all wanted to be just like him. Back in the late 40's, he played for the Detroit Red Wings and was simply known as Mr. Hockey . . . and we were him! In fact, we were whomever we wanted to be, whenever we wanted to be, whomever. I find it amazing that eventually, we were able to develop our own personalities!

While hiding between two parked cars, I could see Joey doing the same, directly across Pine Street.

"D.G., here comes a slow one . . . get ready."

"I'm ready, I'm ready." I shouted back.

Sure enough, it was an old Buick, four-door sedan doing about ten miles per hour, the perfect speed for our encounter. The street was covered with a slick layer of ice while a light snow fall would add to the drama. As the vehicle passed, me and Joey jumped out and grabbed the rear, chrome bumper. There we were, sliding on our goulashes and if everything went well, we could probably get a good, two-block ride. Hopping cars was great fun but, once in a while, things could get a bit nasty. Some cars had terrible exhaust systems that would tend to make you ill or sometimes, you would hit a dry spot (no ice) and crash. Occasionally, if your gloves were wet, they would stick to the chrome bumper and you could go home . . . one glove short. Other times, you could be subjected to what we would call, the wild ride. If a driver would see you attempting to hop his car, he would slow down, make sure you're aboard, step on the gas and take you for the ride of your life! When you would finally let go, you would end up in a pile of snow by the side of the road . . . if you were lucky. One night I ended up underneath a parked car with a number of cuts and bruises. There were many times I would come home with one glove and my Mom would always ask, "Were you hopping cars again?" And I would always answer, "No Ma, Joey's got my other glove!"

During heavy snowfalls, the city would put up barricades so us kids could ride our sleds without fear of being hit by a car. They would "block" West 13th Street from Mahanoy down to Centre Street, and if I remember correctly, that hill was quite steep. We always tried to put at least two guys on a sled because it seemed that the extra weight would make us go much faster. It was probably a mental thing but we were always trying to "push the envelope."

The winter snow also helped us develop some excellent architectural skills for building some great "snow houses." One year, me, Joey, and Donny, built a beauty down on Market Street by Donny's house. It was so large that we were able to make it into a two-roomer! I often wondered why we spent so much time and energy on such a huge project and all I can come up with are these two reasons: 1) to impress a little girl named Shirley, who happened to live in that neighborhood and 2) we needed a private place to smoke and keep warm!

Every year the "city fathers" would bring in a huge Christmas tree and set it up, down-town, on Main Street. I remember that tree being decorated to the nines. Many a cold, wintry night, me and the guys would take a walk downtown just to experience the holiday spirit. And if the weather was permitting, maybe we'd hop a car or two.

During the 1940's, the holiday season in Mahanoy City was unprecedented. Multi-colored lights enhanced the neighborhoods while the aroma of freshly-baked Christmas cookies permeated the cool, crisp air. More often than not, we were graced with an abundant snow fall and that would always remind me of Bing Crosby and his rendition of "White Christmas." And to that, let's add . . . Pauley Phillips' dad. Mr.

Phillips was an electrician and what he constructed in his parlor, every Christmas, was both memorable and magnificent. It was like the back-drop of a wonderful, holiday movie. He would build an entire, miniature community . . . complete with a train station, three model trains, and a number of tunnels. This small town had schools, churches, stores, and family dwellings. It also had workable street lights, small-scale autos, trucks, animals and people. It was surrounded by trees, bushes, and rolling, green hills made from paper mache. The make-believe community consumed the entire parlor! Flip the switch and this fairy-land went into motion. It was unbelievable, and to this day, that little fantasy village has left an indelible imprint on my mind. Thank you, Mr. Phillips, for the wonderful, Christmas memory.

My Dad, who was also pretty handy, made a small yard beneath our Christmas tree as well. It was surrounded with a white, picket fence, some plastic people, old metal cars, and a few small houses to complement our model train. The train was a Marx Electric and the price tag on the box was $3.59! A few years back, Dad gave me the train (still in working order) and I, in turn, passed it on to one of my grandsons. There was many a night when I would fall asleep under that Christmas tree, with cookie in hand, and the train whistling by.

COMMUNITY

❖ ❖ ❖

As you enter Mahanoy City, via the Vulcan Hill, you will be greeted by a large, metallic sign that reads: Birth Of Cable Television. Yes sir folks, cable TV was first established in the United States, in 1948, by Mr. John Walson. John, owner of the local General Electric appliance store, was having a serious problem trying to secure strong and clear television signals from the three major Philadelphia TV stations, primarily because they were being blocked by the mountainous terrain surrounding our little town. After all, how could Mr. Walson sell those fancy black and white TV sets if that picture wasn't up to par? Walson erected a very high antenna on a mountaintop, just south of the borough, and installed a "twin-lead" cable from the antenna to his store and that enabled him to demonstrate a clear, strong signal at his place of business. Eventually, he hooked up several of his customers, who were located along the cables' path, and bingo . . . Mahanoy City became the first community antenna television system (CATV) in the U.S. Now, every time I pay my "cable bill" I'm reminded of John Walson, Mahanoy City, and the Army/Navy football games up at Peca's Coal Company.

Victory gardens, apple orchards, and eating out. The Della Roccas (our landlords on South Street) and our friends, the Capones had the largest and best victory gardens in the neighborhood. They grew everything imaginable, from tomatoes and cucumbers, to lettuce and radishes. Guido Della Rocca also had one of the most productive grape arbors in the area, which enabled him to maintain a substantial stock of good, old "dago red" wine. One particular thing that I remember about Guido and Angelina was their generosity. Whether the home-made wine or the bounty of their garden, they were constantly giving me baskets and jugs to take to my grandparents. Being from the old country (Italy), neither could speak nor understand English very well, but it didn't seem to matter, to me or to them. One other thing. Mr. Della Rocca was the champ when it came to pasta and wine consumption. Dad: Four days a week . . . Della Rocca: Seven days a week! Both he and my Dad lived well into their 90's . . . do you think there's a message here? Guido and Angelina treated me and my family very well during some difficult years back then, and I will never forget them for that.

During WWII, and for years after, victory gardens were growing everywhere. In backyards, vacant lots, municipal parks, and even schoolyards. There were millions of gardens throughout the U.S. and it definitely helped to prevent food shortages. It also helped to build a strong, patriotic morale during that difficult period. Amazingly, about one-third of all vegetables grown in the United States came solely from victory gardens, and don't you know that me and the guys were having a great time just carrying a little salt shaker in our pockets?

Gorman's apple orchard was located on the east end of town just outside the borough limits. If my memory serves me correctly, it was a dark and spooky place, much like a cemetery but with rows of trees instead of tombstones. One night . . . me, Joey, and Donny decided it would be nice to heist a few apples so we made our way up to the orchard. Old man Gorman was somewhat of a mean sort and didn't like anyone, especially kids, trespassing on his property. We figured if we were quiet enough, he wouldn't even know we were there. Well, we were right. He didn't know we were there, but his dog sure did! It had been quite a while since our last visit to the orchard and, believe it or not, we had completely forgotten about the mutt. I guess in todays vernacular, you might say, . . . *"You just can't fix stupid!"* Gorman came busting out of his old shack, flashlight in hand, and began hollering, "You kids get the hell out of my orchard . . . get out . . . get out!" As you can understand, we didn't shout back because we were too busy trying to accommodate his wishes. And then BAM!! . . . a shotgun blast that pierced the silence of the night! We raced through the orchard not knowing whether we were sweating or bleeding. When we finally found a lighted area, we noticed that one of us was in deed, bleeding. Donny had about a two-inch gash on his forehead, just above the right eye, and we figured he probably ran into a low-lying tree branch while making our escape. Donny tied his tee shirt around his head, grabbed a near-by piece of wood (sword), and made like one of those Arab guys in the movies. I believe that was our last trip up to Gorman's, but for me, I will never forget that shotgun blast and how it transformed the three of us into world-class Olympic sprinters . . . in the darkness of night!

As I review those early years of my life, I cannot remember one time when we, as a family, went "out to eat" at a restaurant. For whatever the reason, it just wasn't part of our lifestyle. Occasionally, Mom would take me and my little sister to George's Ice Cream Parlor for a special treat, but that was it. During the 1940's, I'm sure that money was a major factor and eating out was probably prohibitive as compared to eating at home. Especially if you had a large family like the Fazios. I think Joey and Louie had about eleven kids in their household! Hats off to Mom and Dad Fazio for retaining their sanity. Anyhow, me and the guys seemed to be content with our version of eating out: Sitting on the curb while having an apple or an orange.

*   *   *   *   *

Mahanoy City, Pennsylvania is about one mile long and a half-mile wide. It is surrounded by green, rolling hills that, at one time, were loaded with large deposits of valuable, anthracite coal. The borough is located approximately 100 miles northwest of Philadelphia and was part of an extensive rail system which allowed for the expedient dispersal of the "black stuff." Having so many underground coal veins, properties within the community became quite scarce and most residential homes in the valley were restricted to a width of 12.5 feet. Most were three stories high, two or three rooms deep, and would share a "party or common wall" with their neighbor. Practically all of the homes in Mahanoy City were constructed in this manner and "row house" soon became a common term. One negative aspect to row house construction though, was the fact that fire could wipe out an entire block if not immediately subdued. On Memorial Day, 1945, one such fire was set by an arsonist and resulted in the worst fire in Mahanoy City's history. One house, that was not a row house, was Kaier Mansion.

The mansion stood prominently on a small rise and was surrounded by a black, wrought iron fence that caged a couple of large Great Danes. Whenever I would walk downtown and pass the mansion, I would cross to the other side of the street out of respect for and fear of, those "little" puppies. Sixty-three years later I stayed at the Kaier Mansion after it was purchased and re-opened as a Bed & Breakfast, and yes, the fear was gone . . . and so were the dogs!

In later years, music became a very interesting part of my life and for that, I would like to thank MCHS Band Director, William Becker. He got me started on the clarinet and tenor sax, and he also got Joey started on the drums. Who knew that a couple of street kids could eventually rise to that level of sophistication. I want to tell you, Mr.Becker was, without a doubt, one of the toughest task masters I have ever faced . . . but he will always have my deepest respect for his musical knowledge and his ability to instruct the youth of his community.

I can't even think of music without the inclusion of the Dorsey Brothers. Tommy and Jimmy were born in Shenandoah, and their father was a coal miner turned music teacher. Their music was on the level of the great Glenn Miller and they were a pleasure to listen and dance to. Jimmy played alto sax and clarinet while his older brother played trombone and on occasion, some trumpet. One of their favorite hang-outs was the Lakewood Ballroom down at that special place called "The Lake." That little patch of paradise where the coal miners and their families could cool off, relax, and dance to the swinging sounds of the Dorsey Brothers' Band.

John Goepfert . . . another prime example of an exceptional individual. Not only was he capable of building small-town, high school basketball players into competitive professionals, he also had the interest to include and involve himself with the borough's less talented, average kids like myself. Again, like William Becker . . . tough but fair. I remember when I finally got to my freshman year at MCHS, I noticed I didn't have any particular talent on the basketball court but I could play a mean game of H-O-R-S-E. Hey, it was tough holding up your shorts while dribbling! Chances were looking very good that I would NOT be making my way to the NBA. But Coach Goepfert was well aware of me, and most of my buddies, and formed an intramural league to keep us off the streets. It gave us something else to do at night and it beat the hell out of going up to Gorman's orchard! With people like this directing the youth of the community, you really had to try hard to fail.

Another guiding force that helped us through those terrible teens were the porch dwellers. Almost every row house in Mahanoy City had a front porch that was equipped with a glider, or a couple of chairs with a small table. With the exception of the winter months, almost every night after supper, the majority of the population would take their place outside to watch, and sometimes record, the activities of the night. There were many times that me and the guys would hear, "You better put those rocks down or I'll be telling your father!" Now this was "community policing" at its finest! With neighbors like these and a cadre of dedicated educators, growing up in Mahanoy City was in deed, a pleasure.

And who could forget the Teen Canteen? It was located mid-town on Centre Street and I think it used to be the old Merchants Bank. I don't really know if it was donated to the city or if they were paying rent, but whatever . . . it was another great idea. There were pool tables, a ping-pong table, girls, refreshments, a dance floor on the second level, girls, and scattered tables and chairs to relax and shoot-the-breeze. Oh, and there were girls there too! If I am not mistaken, teachers from the community would volunteer as chaperones to keep their misguided teens on track. They had us covered, and you know what . . . this community really cared for its youth!

*　*　*　*　*

While running the streets and having my usual good times, I was completely unaware of two situations that were about to dramatically disrupt my family's future. A while back, my Uncle Babe married Elvira Marina and shortly thereafter, they had a son named Alfie. As you can imagine, the house had become a little over-crowded and daily tensions were on the rise. It's probably why they created the term: Single-family dwelling! Well, one thing led to another, and in short order . . . we were looking for a place to live. And, at roughly the same time, the second shoe dropped. My Dad, and many of his friends, lost their jobs at the Peca Coal Company! This was about 1950 and the coal industry was beginning to unravel. The timing was terrible and the bottom line was this: No job, no money coming in, and no place to hang our hat!

MR. & MRS. DELLA ROCCA   DAD, MOM, & PALMA

AUNT MARY, DAD, MOM,
UNCLE PAULEY, PALMA, &
COUSIN EDDIE DI MARINO

DAD & UNCLE
PAULEY

CENTRE ST. - MAHANOY CITY

MY HOME AWAY FROM HOME

THE EAST END PARK

MAHANOY CITY HIGH SCHOOL

ROW HOUSE EXAMPLE

JOHN GOEPFERT & NORM JONES (MENTORS)

THE WEST END

Mom and Dad soon found a place on Pine Street, down on the west end of town. Man, this place was a dump! I think the rent was like fifteen bucks a month, and believe me it wasn't worth five. Besides, all my friends were on the east end of town. You know, I don't remember anyone asking me what I thought! Anyhow, this place looked like it had been snatched from an old Peter Lorre horror movie. The window pane in the front of the house was cracked, the wooden floors creaked and were in disrepair, the linoleum in the kitchen was ugly and damaged, the wallpaper was peeling in the bedrooms, and a paint job was sorely needed. Practically all of the light fixtures were of the "pull-string" variety and the place was dark, damp, and dreary. The prior tenants even left a few pictures hanging in the parlor. I don't even want to start on the cellar! The habitat also had an offensive odor which was not the scent of Pine-sol. On the plus side, we did have a front porch so Mom could get a good view of the neighborhood and the people in it.

Can you imagine a house with a two-party telephone line and no water heater? Well I can. We shared our telephone number with our neighbors . . . one ringy dingy for the Kapusnicks and two ringy dingys for us. So much for privacy. When it came to bath time, Mom would put a large, round, metal tub in the middle of the kitchen floor, load up the coal burning stove, and transfer containers of hot water to the tub. The key to this community bathing technique was speed. The faster you got in and out of the tub, the more people could get washed without starting the process all over again. It was a bit primitive and took a little time, but it worked. There was nothing quite like heating up bath water on a red hot coal stove during the months of July and August.

Dad, and a couple of his buddies, soon found work in Birdsboro, Pa. which was about sixty miles south of Mahanoy City. Dad's Model A Ford was about twenty years old at the time, so transportation became a problem. They ended up hitch-hiking to Birdsboro on Sunday evenings, shared a hotel room during the week, and returned on Friday nights. They worked at a foundry down there and by the time they paid their hotel and food bill, I'm guessing there wasn't a whole lot of money left. Dad started drinking heavily on the week-ends (and probably during the week) and I could see him and Mom slowly drifting apart. Sadly, I could see it, but couldn't do anything about it. These were tough times for all of us. You might ask, "How tough was it?" Well, it was so tough that Mom started putting "tuna fish" in the sauce instead of ground beef! That's how tough it was. By this time in my life, I was so sick and tired of marinara sauce that Mom began making my pasta with butter and olive oil. Man, what a treat that was. Actually, the butter wasn't really butter . . . it was oleo-margarine, but I didn't sweat the small stuff. *"Mom, I love you, even though you made me eat the marinara sauce when Dad was home!"*

Directly behind our west end estate was the West Palm Gardens. A night club/dance hall that was usually packed on the week-ends and whose bands would keep me awake to all hours of the night. I've always loved music, but this was ridiculous! The constant pounding of drums totally eradicated any semblance of melody. Another thing I remember about the West Palm Gardens was a Saturday afternoon when me and Donny Heckler had in our possession, a cherry bomb. We lit it off, threw it into the dance hall, and ran as fast as we could down Mahanoy Street. Honest to God, it sounded like an artillery shell going off in Europe! I'm assuming that was my infantile retaliation for all those sleepless nights on West Pine Street. What else could it be?

When exiting the rear door of our new humble abode, you entered our back yard. The space was approximately six feet deep and two "row houses" wide. It was all concrete and the side and rear walls were a minimum of two stories high! There was room enough for three clothes lines and that was it. It didn't take too much of an imagination to conclude that this dump on West Pine was a "fire trap!" If, God forbid, we or our neighbors were to have a fire towards the front of the house . . . it would be ciao bambino! As you can probably guess, we never had a barbeque in the back yard.

Almost every Sunday night, when Dad was heading out to Birdsboro, he would remind me of my "duties" while he was gone. Make sure the icebox pan did not overflow and make sure Mom always had a full bucket of coal so she wouldn't have to go into the cellar. And in my spare time, take a couple of burlap sacks and walk the railroad tracks in search of any pieces of coal that may have fallen from the coal cars. Aw yes, the old icebox. During this particular time, we were not really wealthy enough to own a refrigerator, therefore, an icebox it was. Besides, having a refrigerator in this dump would most likely project us into the oxymoron category! Every few days, the ice man would come by and Mom would purchase a block (for about a quarter), have him put it in the upper compartment, and we were set. The lower compartment was for the perishable goods, and as the days went by, the block of ice would melt, and gravitate through a tube, into a pan at the bottom of the icebox. And that was job number one.

Again, primitive, but effective. Occasionally, if the ice man was in a good mood he would toss me a few ice chips, and on a hot day, there was nothing better.

I did not like my second job! The unfinished cellar was a damp, dark, spooky place and that's where the coal bin was. That was also where our resident rats were living! Believe me, every time I went down the cellar, I always made a lot of noise hoping they would run and hide. Many times they didn't. The light in the cellar was one of those pull-chain types with the exposed bulb and one Monday, while going down to fill the coal bucket, I pulled the chain right out of the socket and that left me the rest of the week filling the coal bucket while trying to hold a flashlight and wondering if the rats were watching! The only good thing about having a few rats around was that occasionally, you would hear the snap of a rat trap, and chances are you caught one. I often wonder why we didn't have a cat!

Like the ice man, the coal man came by sporadically to check our coal supply. During the 40's and 50's, most of the houses in Mahanoy City were burning coal and most had cellars with coal bins. A coal bin was a semi-enclosed storage area, near the front of the house, with a window availability. The coal truck would pull up to the curb, open the cellar window, and hook-up a coal chute to the opening. He would then release the coal from his truck, into the chute, and it would tumble into the bin. Yea, I know . . . kinda primitive, but workable. I often wondered if any of those resident rats ever got caught under that avalanche of anthracite? Probably wishful thinking.

Of all three jobs, my favorite was walking the railroad tracks searching for those "black diamonds." I would get in touch with Joey and Donny and we would usually make an afternoon of it. But sometimes, we would end up at the swimming hole and conveniently forget about the task at hand . . . and think about, tomorrows another day.

*   *   *   *   *

Little by little, I began to get used to the west end of town, and if memory serves me, there was a race track at the West End Park primarily for "midget car" racing. But once in a while, Joie Chitwood would bring his "Thrill Show" into town to the delight of his many coal region fans. Joie was kinda like Evel Knievel but leaned more to the entertainment side, rather than the daredevil stuff. I believe there was also an occasional "demolition derby" to help pique the patrons interests. I must say, for a rather small coal mining town, there was always plenty to do.

Every now and then, my Aunts Annie and Mary (Mom's sisters), would stop by for a visit, have a cool glass of beer, and reminisce about the kids. I remember my Uncle Babe used to jokingly refer to them as the "Andrewski Sisters." Aunt Annie would take me in one hand and carry a small, shiny bucket in the other and we would head to a little tavern on the corner of West Pine and 6th Street. I used to love that. It was like, *"Hey, where are you going with that bucket?"* . . . *"Well, I'm going down to the corner saloon to get me a bucket of beer!"* For some reason, I really thought that was funny. Maybe you had to be there.

Living on the west end of town and having my friends on the east end, was a bummer. I was now a freshman in high school and it was relatively easy meeting kids from all over the borough, but I still didn't like it. Eventually though, I was able to meet some guys like Sonny Olin, Frankie Pangonis, Tony Cook, Eddie Lesko, and Marco Markusky, and we all seemed to hit it off pretty well. We would spent a lot of time hanging out at Klipola's Sporting Goods (pool table in the back room), and I soon found myself not going up to the East End quite as often as before. Sonny Olin's dad worked for, or owned, a Hudson dealership outside of town, and got to bring one home every night.

He used to park them in front of his house and me and Sonny would sit in the back seat and play the role like we were a couple of rich guys. What a crack-up. Thinking back, the interior of those Hudson Hornets were all done up in a maroon, crushed velvet, similar to the inside of a coffin! When I think of it today, it was scary . . . back then, we thought it was funny.

Frankie Pangonis was a stand-up guy that turned out to be a good friend and always seemed to be there when needed. He reminded me of the gang on the East End and that made my move a little easier.

One day, while talking to Marco Markusky, I was invited to go on a Good Friday outing which some of the West Enders held every year. There would be about four or five guys, everyone would bring a lunch, and they would spend the day running, jumping, and laughing in the plush, green hills surrounding the borough. Marco did mention that he was going to bring his .22 caliber rifle along just in case we ran into any bears! We both laughed and went our separate ways. When I arrived at home, I asked Mom if I could go on the outing with the guys, and without thinking . . . I told her about the gun! What a dunce. With Dad working out of town, I thought maybe I could blow this one right by her, but it didn't quite turn out that way. She said she would have to call Dad to get his permission and I said fine . . . but don't tell him about the gun. That evening, she called and one of the first things out of her mouth was, "And one of the boys was bringing a gun." I couldn't believe it! Well, that was the end of that game. Under no circumstances would I be going on this outing, whether I liked it or not. I was really upset but I had no one to blame but myself. When would I ever learn to keep my big mouth shut?

During the week before Good Friday, I ran into Marco and he asked if I was going to go. I explained my stupidity and he laughed and said, "Maybe next year." Little did I know that Marco would not be attending next year's Good Friday outing. Marco's rifle had accidentally gone off and the bullet had entered below his chin and lodged in his brain. Marco died a little later at Locust Mountain Hospital! I was numb with sadness and grief, and if it wasn't for good old Mom and Dad, I would have been there and who knows how that would have turned out? From that moment on, when Dad said jump . . . I said, how high? Things were not looking too good for the Di Giamarino family. We were living in a dump, low on money, Mom and Dad were not getting along too well, and I had just lost a friend in an unbelievable gun accident. I was not liking the trend.

*   *   *   *   *

One ringy dingy, two ringy dingys . . . yep, that was our special, two-party telephone line. On this Sunday afternoon, in July of 1951, Mom and Dad were sitting on the front porch and Mom shouted, "Sonny, can you get the phone?" I responded and the voice on the other end said, "Hi Sonny, this is your Aunt Stella from Cleveland, is your Dad home?" Dad came in to take the call and I took his place on the porch. In a matter of minutes, Dad rejoined us and gave us the news: Aunt Stella's husband, Frank Georgiana, had an executive position with a major brewery in Cleveland and he had a job available for Pop, but he could only hold it for a couple of weeks. He needed an answer within a day or two so a decision had to be made, posthaste. Back in the late 40's, thePolidores decided to leave Pennsylvania and build a new life in Cleveland, Ohio. Well, all left except Uncle Danny, and his family, who spent their entire life in Shenandoah and my Godmother, Aunt Irene, and her family, who remained in Philly until moving to Cleveland in or around 1957. Cleveland had jobs and it turned out to be a positive experience for the Polidores . . . but would it be the same for us?

If there would have been a vote, it probably would have gone something like this: Me . . . *no move,* Mom . . . *no move,* Sister . . . *no move,* and Dad . . . *move.* The vote would have been 3 to 1 in favor of *no move,* but we lost! Later that evening, Dad called Aunt Stella and Uncle Frank to inform them that "we" accepted and thanked them for the offer. Dad would leave tonight, hitch-hike to Birdsboro, and give them a week's notice. He would return on Friday evening, sell his car, and tie up any loose ends prior to our departure on Sunday. In the meantime, Mom could sell almost everything we had and be ready to move by Sunday. Any questions?

This was a time of mixed emotions. Dad knew that if major changes were not made, our chances of getting through these rough times would be minimal. Mom also wanted to see those positive changes, but didn't want to leave her family in Pennsylvania. I'm sure my sister agreed with Mom, and that left me. Like Dad, I knew major changes had to be made to insure the survival of the family, but how could I leave my friends? Let's face it, at age fifteen I was not very sure whether I would ever be able to duplicate the friendships I had made in the coal region . . . especially in a big city.

Our final week in Mahanoy City was filled with anticipation and sadness. With the help of my little sister, Mom was in the process of selling all of our "valuables" except for her bedroom set, cedar chest, my bicycle, kitchen ware, washing machine, and clothing. I was busy spending most of my time up on the East End expressing my good-byes and wondering if me and the guys would ever meet again. Later that week, Mom told me that Dad had sold the car to one of his drinking buddies, so it looked like we were in pretty good shape come moving day. Now let me tell you about the car. It was a black, 1930 Model A Ford, two-door sedan, and my Dad bought it in 1940 for $50. He drove it for about ten years and sold it in 1951 for . . . $100! Now that's Jewish.

Finally, Sunday had arrived and so did my Uncles Denver and Freddie, along with my cousin Eddie Di Marino. Their trip from Cleveland was good. Uncle Denver was Aunt Emma's husband and you met my Uncle Freddie earlier. They pulled up to the curb around 8:00 A.M. in Uncle Denver's black, 1949 Mercury, four-door sedan, towing a small trailer. It didn't take very long to load up and we were ready to move out by 9:00 A.M. Everyone said their final good-byes to the Di Labios, a few good neighbors, and then we began to roll eastward on Mahanoy Street. Before we knew it, we were passing by The Bucket of Blood, Price's Potato Chips and Pretzels, Joey and Louie's house, Maff's Service Station, and were about to climb the Vulcan Hill. It was here that I would get my final glimpse of the East End Park as my Mom and sister began to sob. In fact, my eyes seemed a little teary as well . . . must have been a speck of coal dust.

We headed north to the Pennsylvania Turnpike and then west to Cleveland, Ohio. The trip would take anywhere from seven to eight hours. For me and my family, this was a new and scary adventure . . . an adventure that simply began with: A Telephone Call From Cleveland.

UNCLE PAUL
POLIDORE

UNCLE DANNY POLIDORE & DAD

UNCLE FREDDIE POLIDORE

MR. & MRS. DANNY
POLIDORE

AUNT IDA
POLIDORE

AUNT ANNA & TOM GREINER

AUNT STELLA & IDA

AUNT STELLA

AUNT
STELLA

MOM

AUNT IRENE

LOCAL SODA   NICE HAT, POPS

FRIEND, DAD, UNCLE FRANK
GEORGIANA, & UNCLE FREDDIE

EPILOGUE

The turnaround was remarkable! Our life began to take on a new and welcomed meaning. Dad now had two jobs, full-time at the brewery and a part-time gig at Harvey's Moving and Storage. I even picked up a job at Ralph De Caesar's Grocery Store. And as a sidebar, something special happened to good, old Pop . . . he practically stopped drinking! Now here was a guy that could really throw them back but, much to our liking, that game was over. We rented a large, clean, three bedroom house (with hot, running water) on Madison Avenue, near West 73rd, next door to Aunt Mary and Uncle Nunzio . . . the Di Marinos. Of their family of six, only Ferdinand, Albert, and Eddie, were living at home, and they kinda showed me the big city ropes.

In September of 1951, I headed for West High School down on Franklin Boulevard and my sister Palma, started school at St. Coleman's Parochial. On my first day of school, I was fortunate enough to meet Eddie and Danny Vacca (twins) and being "accepted" did not seem to be a problem due to the fact that my last name ended in a vowel. I was smack in the middle of an Irish/Italian neighborhood and believe me, that was a definite plus. Almost every night of the week you could find me either hanging on the corner of West 65th and Detroit Avenue or at The Sweet Shoppe on West 85th and Lorain. In Mahanoy City, I was an "A" student but, with the pressing new environment . . . my grades began to drop like a rock. There was really no good reason to take my text books home at night, if my ultimate goal was to be standing on the corner . . . watching all the girls go by! Besides, any spare time would probably be spent on the Cleveland Indians or the Cardiac Browns. Who could ask for anything more?

The names of Joey, Louie, Donny, Kerry, and Rupe were eventually eclipsed by Frank Santora, Dick Darenzo, Eddie Atkinson, and the Vacca Brothers . . . but were never to be forgotten. We had times in Mahanoy City that could never be duplicated, and those times will always remain as the cornerstone of my childhood memories.

The decision to move to Cleveland was, without a doubt, the correct one. It gave us a chance for a new beginning, which at the time, we sorely needed. Our many thanks go to Aunt Stella and Uncle Frank Georgiana for that welcomed and fortunate phone call, and to the rest of the Polidores for making us feel like family. Yes, Mom still missed her family, but every few years we would return for a visit, and would always take a little side trip to New Jersey to see Dad's bio brothers and sisters.

It wasn't too long before we were able to replace some of our well used furniture, buy our first TV set (a halo light, black and white Sylvania), purchase a 1951 Chevy Sedan, and get a private (one ringy dingy) telephone line. And shortly after that, Mom got an "automatic" washer and dryer (on credit) from Sears Roebuck and Dad opened up a savings and checking account at the local bank. Now this is life as it should be. I was so deeply delighted to see my family, so close to destruction ... so joyfully reignited.